To the Bone

saturnalia books

Saturnalia Books
13 E. Highland Ave., 2 Floor
Philadelphia, PA 19118
info@saturnaliabooks.com

ISBN: 978-0-9818591-1-8
Library of Congress Control Number: 2008936646

Book Design by Saturnalia Books
Printing by Westcan Printing Group, Canada

Cover Art: *Still Life with Rabbit and Pheazant* by Snejana Slavova

Distributed by:
University Press of New England
1 Court Street
Lebanon, NH 03766
800-421-1561

I would like to thank Mark Doty and Henry Israeli not merely for selecting the book but also for their great editorial advice. Two remarkable students read earlier drafts of the manuscript and offered invaluable comments. Eoin Burke's accurate insights were characteristically frustrating but very helpful. Giaco Furino understood like few how incompatible kitchen and poem often are and helped me reconcile them. Thanks also to my parents for their support and my deep gratitude to my teachers.

For Katharina and Madeleine

Contents

But the cook isn't listening
he knows all feasts are delusions, that the scent of immortality
and the savor of oblivion are one, that both give of
the whiff of something rancid.
                                        —Larry Levis

I

Artichoke

Somewhere, the downy bristles of its heart
stand for our hungers, for our wants.
Somewhere its shingled leaves explain
God or nature's intractable math.
Chef's tasting offers adobo-crusted tuna
on a barigoule of turned artichokes.
To turn, you swivel the vegetable,
paring blade perpendicular to the base,
till grayish exterior gives way to green.
That's as far as any book has taken me,
abridged directives, know-how, aside.
The rest is up to nerve and muscle,
when it's too late. Not just late to learn,
midnight almost. With nine cases to go,
better take Chef's advice and not dwell
on each heart more than ten seconds.
"They better be round," he means round,
means literal one Mississippi, two Mississippi
kind of second and the heart is bract
and pulpy calyx, bobbing in acidulated water.
Poets of the 1890's got high on opium
drunk on absinthe, just to read the shimmer
spume, and fluorescence of a worn-out world.
Poets now will diet on bizarre produce.
Furrowed between bad childhoods
and worse divorces, curly tuber and thistle,
pomegranate and alligator pear are harvested
and piled high in altars to a faith—
untenable and dubious, like all faiths—
that any subject, scraped from so much

of the anthropocentric dung that manured
its growth, will lock the senses to
a primal world, Edenic, Paradisal.
Butcher will pity the sow's frown,
carpenter know tree from a planned stud.
And cook? Well, Rosa, helping me tonight,
lit two votive candles in the morning.
Her kid hasn't eaten since her husband left,
and she's wondering if something she did,
moonlighting here and there, overtime,
alienated Javier, though she doesn't say
alienate. She's ambling the corridors
of perplexity and as she goes, she christens
the new turns in a place too ready to aerate.
Like Eve in the garden, food's her least concern,
though she knows food, with that carnal intimate
knowledge that lets her talk and scramble
through each case, an artichoke every three
seconds, perfectly round, three literal seconds.

Prayer

(From a catalog for Masters of 17th Century Genre Painting)

No art, no mirrors, no rich brocade.
Father, mother and son are hiatus
from men in slashed sleeved jackets

and girls corseted in silk
strumming a motet while a maid
lifts a ewer, holds a lap dog

or just stands on guard. In Jan Steen's
Prayer Before the Meal, light slants
against the wall, but doesn't bounce

with that pristine quality one finds
in Vermeer and Der Hooch.
The room is grimed. No jewels,

no scarlet drapes to backdrop leisure,
no maps to hem the territory which
parceled and torn bought the cloth

for the drapes, gold for the filigree
and time to flirt and serenade.
The mother must have spruced up

the rough brass chandelier with
a dried up branch. The father might
have nailed a scroll calligraphied

with chapter and verse to the wall.
But that's it for embellishment.
The ceramic jug rests on a bench.

The barrel is barely draped with
a burlap rag. Everything is moored
to the dock of the quotidian.

Their ham's more gristle than meat.
And yet they thank. Gray jacket, white
cap and collar, she sits below the open

window with her young child on her lap.
Across the table, he holds a winter cap
and bows his head as if to sort

the beguilement droughts and land-
lords into a map larger than the tilled acre
and the section line. With neighbors –

wealthier women and more powerful
officers—they share perspective,
tone and brushstroke, laws in whose

pruned eloquence they seem dark
impossible stumps. As color, they're all
gray and black. If they'd be speech, though,

they'd be not roughcasts of an original
meaning, not words eddying from
the tongue of saint or poet to spiral down

some Godly cochlea, but sounds that
imitate and echo the world's music,
itself an anagram of fact:

utterance with no rhetoric,
sounds apt only to need: to conjure
and plea, to complain and pray.

The Smell of Cooking

The smell of cooking can evoke an entire civilization.
— Fernand Braudel

Let the sweet of roasting almonds be
the minaret, the muezzin calling, Averroes;

the kindling of tandooris down on Chestnut,
the temple kingdoms of medieval India;

and steam from the rice-cooker, stupa,
incense rising, dams flooding a paddy.

The smell of garlic from the take-out
near the station was acrimony for a while,

resentments carried over
from a sum too volatile in these blocks:

The owners and a bunch of kids,
the former swinging at them with a bat,

the latter taunting back, some with bricks
pried from the sidewalk, some with sticks.

It was mainly air, a hoedown, letting out
the small annoyances that had pent up:

the pilfered candy bars and scribbled walls.
So garlic filled the block, caught a wind,

blew down Pulaski and Queen Lane
and like a gloss too vast to understand

explained at least the squad car on the curb
but also, even maybe, as some people say,

some clogged arteries and hurried lives,
the break down of the nuclear family,

assimilation, too. Don't forget
the Styrofoam littering the playground.

Yes that. And more: the railroad
lines and robber barons. Slip in also

the vertical axle of Chinese windmills.
Let the lamb in grape leaves mean

the hollow blades of scissors in Istanbul;
let *Pho* waft the three rising galleries

devoted to Vishnu in *Angkor Wat*.
Delete the *Escorial* insert a *sofrito*;

cut Versailles and paste *beurre blanc*.
What value could one insert for say

a Middle Passage? Jerk paste, *fufu*?
And for the American Century

as public television likes to call
the 20th or the 21st supply what?

A double-decker cheeseburger?
A Pizza? Pulled pork?

Would garlic do, issuing from
a grimed, graffitied wait-space

no larger that a tool-shed? For a while
it was redolent of nothing but what it was:

the root's ammoniac moisture rising,
covering up the dumpsters' caustic stink.

Let the mustard oils of cabbage cooking
be the inlaid Minabar of the Almoravids.

To some I guess the whiff of burning ram
means a covenant that left the signees homeless,

wandering and wailing, grub and foray
for promised lands that kept a caravan intact.

To others, catch the smoke of fat melting,
its column, architrave, entablature.

Caesar's armies won the *Pax Romana*
on a diet beasts would cough at, Shakespeare says,

the stale of horses and the gilded puddle.
But then, what should we make of this

a meal so freakish, so fairytaleish
like a demented ark it took every animal

Roman chefs could get their hands on,
all de-boned but with their structures whole.

Calf went into cow; piglet into sow;
ewe into lamb, seasoned, extremity to extremity.

Then like some riddle moving through clues,
the cooks worked down to fowl, goose,

duck, squab, all plucked and de-boned
and seasoned also, all waiting for

the smaller animal inside, till all there was
was tern or sparrow, something small enough

to cradle a white truffle and the cooks
proceeded to truss each cavity and roast

the whole concoction days on end.
The wicked gods, of course, the false cults,

as Augustine asserts, but also this kind
of ostentation made the transubstantial flesh

a deal, and let *Christi corpus sumite,*
caro cibus sanguis potus be diet for millennia.

Let the garlic frying in the wok be
the broken peasantry of the Han, T'ang and Sung,

five generations who rose from coolie
to entrepreneur, closed on the corner store

paid for the deli, the cleaners, the take-out
and as Tu Fu said *Ch'i and Lu lost to view*,

instead the projects looming behind.
In front, a payroll to command, none white,

some blacks, some Mexicans to haul
and Chinese only to mince and peel,

to steam the rice, slit the boxes and stir in
the cans. Oyster sauce, hoi sin, sweet and sour

bubble up on contact, coat sprout, pepper,
floret, pea; their steam gets sucked

up the exhaust and travels down Wayne Ave.
That's one cuisine, one civilization down,

wafting its wisdom round section eights
with *fan-cai* and *qi* and infusing derelict

Victorians and boarded carriage houses
with its deep-seated, Mencian certainties,

that those who work are to be ruled
by idle Mandarins. Let it be then the Mandarins

and how they pit working against poor,
poor against working, so the gust of stir-fry

told a parent the take-out opened
and he went in to clear the air, settle the score.

What happened to the Roman feast?
The host and his three guests tossed the meat,

split the truffle. And more immediate,
what happened at the take-out?

The usual exchange, an inarticulate
quibbling about who or what was right

or wrong, the owners/ the kids,
then, the usual words clambering through

slur and insult to see who mounts the highest.
From here on, it's just hear-say,

someone knocking down the altar
the owners kept with fresh fruit every day,

someone stepping from the bullet-proof
compartment that guarded register

and kitchen. Bullets? A red-hot wok? Fire?
Some *denouement* that has choppers

hovering overhead like vultures on accident,
and the network cutting from the numbers

propped by empty shells to some mother,
black or Chinese crying her son or husband's

death and then, the whole "community"
black or Chinese, reenacting the same

photogenic exercises in grief, candle vigils,
the dispossessed at their photo-op crying

or protesting for the instant an editor will fit
them there, loose change between the riches

of A list weddings and divorces:
The American century, that sulfurous whiff,

the chemical stench of fires traveling,
don't matter what cooked there.

Expulsion

If the punishment was to make ends meet
then they have the whole classified page,
can circle management, service, the stage,
and suck the free-market of its sweets.
If sweating's what it was really about,
the range spewing hundred eighty thousand
BTU's combined should be plenty to amend
and still the cook shows up, clocks in and out.
If when the fruit gave in, knowledge leached
like gossip from overripe neighbors on stoops,
why didn't the dark or dirty secrets teach
a master plan, the news of how to reach
success, identify the breaks and loop-
holes, tell why the wayward don't get rich?

Honest

He'd scowl at me with an ugly toothless grin,
after I'd dump the fifteen pans into his sink.
Someone would whisper "Princess Lea,"
and Leo'd kick a bucket or throw the hose
against the back-splash and then disappear.
The scar on his left cheek had tanned too long
to blame any barbwire he'd crawl under
though I pictured an exodus with him some place—
Piedras Negras, Eagle Pass—and imagined him
a bad childhood on top of that, a father,
drunk and tired, stuck in some shanty town,
scarring him with a stick, or belt, or fist.

The thing about the poor in poems is
they seem too close to those beggars Murillo
and Velasquez propped on curbs or sheds.
Lurid, beautiful, but ultimately left-over
oils from the portrait of some royal brat.
Maybe I'm wrong and every time a painting
or poem sketches a scrub pad soaked with solvents
and weathering the knuckles to dry cracks,
there is some assay at pity and compassion,
a stab at exposing the master while wrenching
some archetypal martyrdom of someone's life.

One thing I know, Leo would spit the fake
green-card I'd given him, the abusive father,
the childhood town, its white-washed walls
pock-marked with the bullet holes of insurgence,
bleeding the dried piss of the drunk soldiers

who put the rabble down. Even if I'd invoke
the truth of fiction as deeper and explain
recombinant pasts as garnering a kind of justice,
even if I say the child is father of the man.
Mind always short-changes reality for *a* sense
that's always tragic, always trivial,
and condenses lives that won't reconstitute.

Here's Leo: Chef has run his fingernail
down the grout to dig what crusts there,
show him the grime and, an added bonus,
keep his middle finger shoved an inch
from his nose so he see, so Leo tell if
that's what we call clean and Leo stands,
smiles when it's over, sees me seeing—
that gawk of an outsider stumbling on cult.
My dumb astonishment. That toothless grin
that meant you don't know anything, honest.
And what he whispered.
"Leo's Leo," someone in the background said.

Dishwasher

The nasty what he stirred on breaks,
a tepid, cloudy broth from staff-meal
enriched with trimmings of every kind,
half eaten prime-rib, untouched shrimp,
shreds from joints of duck or squab,
the joints themselves sometimes or gristle.
The whole concoction brined, bloated.
The way he'd scarf up the stuff
from the pan that weltered eight hours,
we figured him a son too prodigal.
But most guys back there, with lives
of overtime hosing dishes, banging crates,
scouring burnt pots, dislodging jammed
disposals, bathed on steam and grease
are prodigal, exiles, five minute bios
of driftings, odd jobs, the three bucket sink
their salt lick. Circumspect, he'd crawl
under and twiddle with the washer's belt,
bang a pipe, tighten a bolt, just to quiet
a bellow or whistle. What did he think
in that thick, sing-song patois no one
in the kitchen understood? His keep,
perhaps. You know those old Histories,
how a border always bristles with stakes?
The woods are dense. Past the palisade,
these guys pet the pelts that cover them,
kindle a fire, worship sap or bough, barbarians.
So Greeks or Romans or whoever chains them,
puts them to dig—a shaft, a ditch, a wonder
of the world which slave-driver's own ravages

will tumble in time. Though, the one to brush
the wreck will tell barbarians soiled the marble,
peed in aqueducts. Well, here's your guy.
Our barbarian. You know the histories?
How they start hundred pages or more
and map faults, ridges, whatever crusted
before settlement, just to log expulsion,
conquest, famine, the pell-mell settlement
fattening. One premise being unless every
fault and gulf be tallied human accident
would be just that; the other, how long
it took those chorographies to set. Like
the emulsion of millennia, Occitania blushed
from its own amethyst to the lavender of France.
Algeria in red, Morocco terracotta,
so pristine, borders saturated, interiors fading.
How blush of one place and plum of another
must scuff when self is smuggled in crossing,
how trips must be like navigating the nuances
of a bruise and destination is echo of what's
left behind, in Mali or the South, bad luck,
death-squads or famine. You know the histories.
Here's their barbarian. I can see him still,
after we broke our stations down and began
to file out or just lingered with the shift's
last business. He'd wash his hands, crouch
on a crate and sup the stuff, that ghastly
stew he scraped from cornucopia's back-end,
as if he knew a home, a permanent address.

Back Alley

Here floodlight elongates the fractal
game of chain-link on the brick wall;
obelisks and pyramids shift and stretch
above the dumpsters, then shrink

as cars on 15th street wrap the night
with the high-speed ribbon of their head-beams.
The pigeon has struggled for hours
stuck in the barrel where we dump the oil.

Its sound would stun a soul mid-step,
make it do like the music from inside,
drift out a moment, gust back
behind the door before it seals.

Here's where we break,
where you find us smoking,
in checkers, clogs and whites
toques sometimes, bloody aprons.

Tourist would think of docks
where smuggled goods arrive,
retrace his steps, find a well lit block
knowing every place has A and B flick,

choose A, unless a girl pin-hammer
her high heels and turn the corner there.
After all, every city's flooded
with conventioneers who

have the smile and hand-shake
that'll sell anything, bearings, soap.
Get them off their booth, shop-talking
trade-secrets over Kamikazes,

by the second round, they're hounding
the bar tender, slipping a twenty to maitre d'
if only he steer them to the right club,
get the stretch-limo to pick them up.

No B flick, backstage maybe, the lambs
come in undressed and dripping,
the fish still rigor in the ice, and money
changes hands. We step out there,

just before we break our stations down,
end of service, when hot-shots close
their deals to cordials and Petit fours.
Between fried morsel and poached bite,

they revisited laws, zoned blocks,
bulldozed a field for a new mall.
No backstage, then, where we smoke,
but the artery to capital's long arm

where its cargo, human or otherwise,
legal or otherwise, arrives; where
nightly, buzz boy empties the heel taps
of handshakes, lets scavenger feed.

Back Alley Revisited

The animal dying is what I steered clear of
one of those pigeons that waddle too near us
in train stations, bus stops, greedy for refuse,
pecking limp fries, nipping trampled stuff.
Someone in a hurry forgot to close the drum
where we dump the fryer's oil every few days
and the bird perched, fell, angling for that stray
burnt squid, a dried-out potato chip, a crumb.
At rest, it buoyed like a seabird on the horizon
then the puffed chest, the flapping, a splatter
without spray, that unctuousness of dream where
the motion of survival fails, and fails again,
that quality of memory writing its *mea culpas*,
knowing its disheartenments will not forgive.

Appetite

America's epic is the Odyssey of appetite

—Campbell McGrath

And there's the signs: a Lotus Dim-Sum near 8th street,
not far from a Helios Steak and Gyros.
    Further down, near the highway ramp
    the mudguard silhouette

of someone's bombshell fantasy glows pink and beckons
into SIRENS, "members only" gentlemen's club.
    Some track letters have lost their bulbs,
    but one can still make out the girl.

Even in those deserted offshoots, hardly city
a factory, a by-pass, the mile on mile of chain link
    that fences in refineries
    warehouses, depots,

a giant Neptune beacons truckers off the ramp.
Call it vintage signage, the neon tridents, the castle,
    the pig's tail wiggling while his spatula
    flips a chop, the flames beneath.

And that's glow only, only the drive-by overview,
the nimble stimuli niggling the retina in its roadside
    outing to buy, buy, buy
    the Coke and fries, the deep-dish.

Downtown, Chefs, praised or panned, old luminaries
and rising-stars constellate their kitchen pass,
    fiddling with sprigs, wiping rims,
    reading dupes from the machine.

And foodies come, drop their keys with the valet,
skip the puddles, hurry sidewalks, not to lose
　　　the reservation, try new twists
　　　on *Cote d'Agneu* or *feijoada.*

The *Siete Mares* salad at their fingertips
is navigable only with the menu's global trawler
　　　which has tangled everything:
　　　smoked Patagonian toothfish,

shrimp, eel, urchin. That's the first course only,
woven and mounded on frissée, topped with
　　　brunoised Poblano pepper
　　　dressed with a plantain vinaigrette,

and served quietly in the half-light which shows-off
the copper exhaust hood, the open kitchen's glow
　　　but hides the sweat of the brigade.
　　　Though they sweat, move and sweat.

After all someone must work for us, culinary
school grads and the Mexicans beneath them.
　　　Someone must storm the ramparts
　　　of appetite with a new dish,

even if there's your occasional Thersites,
darting from the fun, renouncer, nay-sayer.
　　　One I know who swears he's weaned
　　　himself off vegan to raw and is now

considering the move to sun-light diet alone.
Surplus, the make-up that'd compel anyone to kiss
　　　poverty by choice, on the one hand;
　　　on the other, the only thoroughfare

that winds in the ashlar battlements of Argos or Troy.
Tell the Nicaraguans dollying fifty pound sacks
    of Vidalias or Yukon golds
    just to get the invoice signed

barreling from one alley to another so
every joint can have its stuff by noon,
    that they forgo protein and carb,
    that there's injury involved

not just in sty and coop but harvest also.
Tell them to turn Jains mumbling *ahimsa, ahimsa*
    and at best they puzzle through
    your reasoning and still make you for mad.

They'll fill you in on the worry of bad seasons
a bad harvest's pangs and thank that Neptune lit
    at four a.m. when forklifts
    rumble the walk-in warehouses

where they load the produce to their truck.
Tell them the back-doors they unload to are paratactic
    songs, small epics to a much grander cycle,
    an Odyssey—they can talk about returns,

about wars probably, what they do or undo,
about the rueful journeys home, their deceptions
    the frayed loyalties and pains,
    the thanks one gives before a slaughter.

II

Nocturne

What I thought was going on at 3 a.m.
from the comfort of my desk, the privilege
of books, was wrong, no surprise there,
no surprise the all-nighter never slurred
its way to the fluent Baudelairean nasal,
or that the pitch around didn't refine
and show the *condition* or *comédie humaine*,
though both were there, in the steward
carting empties, the operator nodding
by his switchboard, the whole sad list
of tasks and people, Kelly choosing
the shift to sober up; Bruce, doing anything.
Guatemalans sprayed those chemicals
that made grime bubble up on contact.
The old bathroom attendant cat-napped;
concierge knitted scarves and winter-hats;
Joy, behind the sign-in desk did word-puzzles,
till 5:00 am, when they slid their ID's through
the scanner, had the guard check their bags
and walked out, to the tunnel, up the stairs
where it was still dark. Come light of day,
particular existence would bleach them,
nothing, a mob too broken to line up,
with ceremonials to no god but Need,
bilge stuck to traps attesting for them.

Surveillance

None shall escape me and non shall wish to escape me.
                                                    —Walt Whitman

     Walt Whitman, the slipshod demographics
you yapped in endless catalogs still cross the river,

     en masse, as you said, day and night,
though there's no currycomb or tongs or anvils.

     Livery, instead, for the doorman,
the bellboy, the stewards: riding boots also,

     top-hats, toques, French-maid uniforms.
Your Bedowee flags cabs. Your free Cuban

     polishes stainless steel. Uarda, the Croatian
room-service girl, has to skip through tins

     and cords to load the service elevator.
Martín is boss and gets the job he wants.

     Awkward, he says, but turn her on,
get her under control, she glides the floor.

     The buffer is a female, though not solely
on the account that his mother tongue

     will gender every noun. The mind is female
like a vacuum cleaner, and a door.

Go figure, go figure the soul's male
and sugar also, and countries but not fatherlands.

Anyway, Martín is past linguistic subtleties.
Google *Latinas* you'll get a good idea

what type of date *la pulidora* is;
do a whole shift, the whole ground floor

the monogrammed entrance, the lobby,
the rotunda, the ballroom, you figure why

anyone would dream up
a silicone genie to do the *bachata* with.

It can't be that bad, to Amaru and Henry
his underlings, he's left the counters, sideboards,

the casework in the cigar bar. No *pulidora*
for that, just rag and chemicals, just fingering

each fluted keystone, each domed shell,
brassoing the pulls, the hinges, the latch,

polishing the marble tops, till morning
when the place will gleam enough,

Martha will joy stick her cameras trying
to angle out the reflections that saunter

like inverted wet ghosts on her screens.
Bulldoggish, not fifty, she'll hum all night

through the five songs in a row without talk,
no interruptions that her station promises.

She'll hammer the soft ballads,
hop to Eminem and Jay-Z

and here and there, sit up and stare,
sure that Eric and the trash removal guy

are up to no good. The truck will hog the ramp
the two will banter till Sheila rears

through the double doors from pastry
and the trash guy lets a hydraulic whine

to let her know they're watching and they like.
Obscene? Offensive? Martha couldn't care.

She worries that the truck's tank
blocks the west side camera by the loading ramp,

that these guys are there to corner a blind spot
while someone else skims loins and racks.

The walk-ins are pad-locked at night
but Martha knows:

When Guatemalan prep-cooks cough
they cover-up the grating of a hinge;

when Nigerian porters stray from carts,
take inventory at the silver room;

when Russian housekeepers smile,
they served rooms with men and money in them.

She'll tell you. Of the two Thai seamstresses
of Jamaican valets, of Haitian concierges

she has stories, songs of occupations,
one could say, squalid and sleazy like the jobs.

Walt Whitman, sometimes, I think
your hand over-reached and now

by some sick metempsychotic joke,
some karma whittling at the optimism in the song

you've come back Martha, regardless
of soul being male, a woman from Camden,

mother of five, grandmother, and dieting;
sometimes I think you're stuck in her ambivalent

night shift, neither master nor servant.
She has your vista to food, drink, pulse,

wives turning tricks, daughters scrubbing toilets.
The kids of those not rich colored your poems.

They stride her nights in black and white,
faint, grainy, in the low resolution of distrust.

Lockerroom

(Variations on a Theme by Anthony Hecht)

The coltish horseplay in the lockerroom
   is gone, thank God. The jocks get younger,
enough to pity, see their sadist rough
   and tumble for what it is, comeback
to dad who scowled or principal who mocked,
   to beatings, burns or even darker stuff.
The humiliations stay and so their backdrop:
   the lockers where we change to uniform.

It's whites and checks now but the louvered doors
   still breathe the unwholesome stench of sweat
and mildew, still the double-prong hook jams
   and the hasp pull-handle needs a jiggling
for the fourteen gauge brushed steel doors
   to open with that bang which keeps
that dry and hollow resonance of fear.
   Fred, Jerry, Brad, I never thought

they'd pound the doors of memory again
   barge in with antics, beltings, howls.
One kid they dry-humped, another one
   they snapped with towels till his back
welted. They shoved one down a flight of stairs
   next day they made him kneel and beg
then got him on all fours to crawl and shriek
   make me your bitch, make me your bitch.

The coltish horseplay in the lockerroom
   is gone, thank God. Bullies my age
walked management, rose corporate and haul

themselves to places no one down here
has time or money to afford. They work-out
  at gyms, or sauna in private clubs
where ego re-enacts its rivalries
  on different terms, the stocks and cars.

Otherwise José, who bench-pressed six
  hundred pounds, now lolls in with
his uniform, panting because he's carrying
  half the weight he lifted back then.
And Pete, the high school quarterback will tuck
  his gut to button up his vest.
They both will shy and turn around when Troy
  the gray-haired homosexual maitre d'

comes in to wash his hands, adjust his bow-tie,
  both will loosen up when he steps out
with "who's your papi" or "who takes it in the ass,"
  "bend down, grab your ankles, cough."
Phobia or just vestigial habit masking
  how innocuous they've become.
Still unsettled, still binging on days off
  but too wrecked to threaten and raising

hell only because the poor will cling
  to anything they think they own,
the meanness and severity they take
  for strength could be the hub caps, broken
office chairs, torn umbrellas piling
  in the shopping carts of bums.
It's pride or hurt pride, what they need to fit
  the uniform, livery, aprons, boots.

Against Surrealism

I work with a guy who makes sure the horn-tips show
        on the edge of his silk-screened bandana, Diablo is his chosen name;
    a girl with a manhole on her nape, property of some initials, MDB;
            the fish butcher asked me to feel the bullet on his neck
and the man who commands and pays is short, bald, myopic
         and wears, in a sort of back-handed homage to tie-die,
                 pants with squid printed all over them.

He's boss, will wield a limp asparagus right in my face
      and like some crazed Joe Morton hurrying his cargo
         from Inagua to the docks, keep yelling "I wanna see salt."
No synesthesia here, taste prodding sight, sight doing the work of skin.
        Nor did I fish him from dream's pools
             or wade him out of some unconscious swamp
     though the screaming might say father,
        and the limp sword come so near my face...

He'll go awhile, "I wanna see fucking salt. See it understand?"
    "Don't make me bust your balls."
         The maddening, ugly little bastard could be delirium's dwarf
jesting round the tyrannies of need and want; the fears or withdrawals.
        But he isn't, that's the problem, that's my problem
with cows falling out of the sky and landing in the Laundromat's parking lot;
with the dream of the brand new shoes left on the side of the road
        and turning some sort of rough bark peeled from the tree of life;
with names called underwater and bubbling like short-hand for lust or love.

Those abandoned rail yards and more desolate factories in DeChirico
            their painstaking metaphysics are the one skyline
     in my daily nine mile bus ride to work.

So abandonment shattered glass, alienation's boarded windows
mean the dwindling value in my unpaid for house,
mean the debt is still delinquent and a single solar-powered cipher
translates as keep the job, keep the job, keep the job.

For every Lobster telephone receiver, I mound slivered, pickled lamb's tongue
on raw fish; for the unstrung racquets volleying non-existent balls
baby coconuts with the heads of langoustines peering out,
for the melting clocks a scented, salted burning-hot river-rock on a plate beside
deep fried fish-tails, octopus bacon, and raw tuna, at twenty-nine dollars a pop.
Those are the murky seas I swim in nightly, like a hurried diver.

Banquet

It took eight hours to chisel the life-size grizzly bear
from a block of ice forklifted onto the loading ramp
and eight of us to wheel the upright animal and check
its teetering all the way to the Grand Ball Room.

And now, Joe was dislodging the plumber's snake
of a rope and opening the conduit so guests pour
Absolute or Grey Goose, let it run from the head
to the neck to the arm, and binge in the cool liquor

as it funneled out of the extended, welcoming paw.
"It would've been better if they chose his dick,"
was Chef's only take on the enterprise. The *they*
being two twenty-somethings born to two rival firms

but tying the knot anyway and ready to party round
the thing all night. Five hundred guests, two nights,
rooms paid for and also the welcome breakfast,
the lunch, the rehearsal diner, and the next day

breakfast and lunch again, white glove canapés,
the ceremony and the banquet, all game: woodcock
consommé, wild sockeye salmon salad, venison loin.
Big time, big game hunters, someone said.

So the ice grizzly made sense, sort of, at least
in surfeit's intractable logic, in the same way
this Duke or Count, this Renaissance grandee
makes sense, who liked to keep his enemies close

so he embalmed, dressed and sat them at the table.
Abstraction being the historian's job, he chooses
vengeance and dissimulation to explain a reign,
lets the specific scatter on the tables servants swept.

For once management did not white out the total;
for once, they let the identities out of the bag,
how father of the groom golfed with Clinton,
how the bride's step-dad hunted with Dick Cheney

and had pissed from the same blind waiting for elk.
Those finer points were meant to prod a better yield,
meant to let us know what formidable handshakes
kept our paychecks in the same orbits as treaty and bill.

Dissimulation and vengeance,
the in-the-wings, behind-the-scenes backstabbing
we worked under. They'd be in laws so the bad blood
of failed mergers had to be let between the mothers.

They lectured Chef, scolded management, scared
a Sommelier and brought a bartender near tears.
Mixed-signals, conflicting requests, ambiguous orders.
Wait-staff had it worse, like getting round barbwire

in no man's land with crystal on a tray.
Those who chose the war, spooned consommé,
sliced meat, cut cake, and danced to the band,
partied, reveled beneath the bear all night.

After Hours

By the time the jukebox carrousels to E-4
and Springteen screeches something about union fees,
      bad breaks, worse foremen
Jim is too hammered to make out the words,
Andrew too damned tired to care. Or maybe they know
the song's calluses and sweat are capital
      banked at their expense
to pay the loft, fetch a limo for superstars?

Organizer, operator, great ironist,
History has cleaned her records. Otherwise, hiss,
      like gristle on flame,
would date the song, tell how History Herself
obsolesced unions and their dues,
the foremen who ran plants, at least around these parts.
      Still She hums her bad jokes,
great ironist, letting bird go only after

pressing it to stone; keeping all its doings
in past tense, though She must have her rickety
      piles, shantytowns,
bad blocks stored somewhere in the future, and also
in the now, where She unearths the bird, peels
the cartonage of mummies to reveal Sappho's latest
      words [blank] *body old age now*
[blank] *my hair's turned*. Those tacets aren't tacets,

but burrowings, History's obvious and tiresome high jinks,
the missing clues that guard Her clogs and flowcharts
      make them a secret,
a mystery that keeps our ears pressed to burial ground

or battlefield, a shepherd's shack, a ruined castle,
to broken columns, the brick-walls of a rail-yard,
        a high-rise. Like supplicants,
we know Her answer is not exactly no,

but still will flaunt the very things we wished against
the flayings and slaughters, the fires, lootings, wars,
        the assertive gun
and the submissive retreat into our homes.
According to Persian poets it's indecorous
to ask if a thing is fair. To weigh the damage
        of torn branch,
or cry foul because low wage bough boss his goods,

means one's trying to figure the ways of God,
something that can be done only by consorting
        with demons.
Well my buddies here, waitron and saucier
resemble the Persian poets at least in that,
even if the theological breeches of theodicy
        couldn't be further
from their minds, doing shots, grimacing at the lemon,

checking out low cleavages, tank top and tube top.
If the blueprints to utopias have allotted them a room
        they really don't care
"That's stuff just girlie man" lanky post-punk Brad
will say before he swerves to feed another coin
to the machine, presses whatever number
        BANG Sugar BANG
is on and lets "The Machine Gun Song" make its point.

I guess they're partly right, what kind of gear are chiffonade
and concasse if the picks and plough of comrades in Soviet
        posters are any clue?
What's a wine service when that sledgehammer breaks ground?
But even if poster's wrong, if all that looms
in the future, aside from rickety piles, bad blocks,
        is the high-speed
hairpin turn that strips Justice of her the blindfold,

that half-disrobes Her, seeing Her own nakedness,
seeing Her own works, won't sword make the point still;
        still, won't Her minions
doctor scales and pat the working-poor on the back,
send them home with some homiletic on the virtue
of hard work, on the pride of Carpenters, the self-esteem
        of welders, a pipe-fitter's
self-reliance? Isn't a job well done, a new scraper

gracing the skyline because you tight-roped the girder
and ran wire from penthouse to lobby, went back up
        to plug the AC,
something to turn back in pride and tell the kids about?
Something less grandiose, say, the guy who had every jaded
pedestrian gawking because at 17 below,
        he was careening
from second empire scroll to second empire scroll

chipping at a liability which had built up, had become
too obvious to ignore when the "falling ice" signs
        turned inadequate that winter?
What about the unclogged drain, the lube job?
What about the guy who sits all night inside a shed

outside *Glaxo Smith and Kline* guarding a breezeway
      as far as I can tell?
What about us—the three hundred covers, the good sauce?

Well the answer, being History's, isn't exactly no
but being History's is also distorted and corrupt,
      humming in the missing trochee
of a Sappho line, in the drunk clerk's slip of the pen,
in the floors of studios where they cleaned the record's hiss,
and it might be telling why most live to the tic of shifts,
      the working-day's rough metronome,
telling to the defeated secret, good news, interjections.

Alas, these guys don't understand, or care to understand;
they know Her works, the way I got to know this friend who
      hired me to work,
to mix cement, lay tile, job almost done, backtracked on the deal,
locked me out, cheated me, a biblical knowing almost
except the screw's figurative and still she'll wave at me.
      Biblical also
that losers get to judge. Beast will have the final word.

III

Failed Vallejo Translation

His words, like the matter-of-fact, the knobby
everyday, a plough or pick say, will knock a pebble,
skid and tangle in those knotted hirsute weed-roots
that mat the topsoil and keep the season barren.

Theoretical and practical, he'd call the furrow
and plant the beaten peasants there to turn over
stony substratum for surface clod, add morning
fog rising and tugging them through the acreage,

a whole valley, till dusk, when the sacerdotal order
of the bottle doffed its investitures and let the secret
scripture of the waning moon, the public river
roll off their tongue. It isn't what we do with words

but what was done with them by others in the past
that does us in. The pious stick that whipped
and straightened the crooked Indian tongue to pray
garbled Latin and plea in out-and-out Castilian,

made him write *telluric, hierarchical.*
Still his miners come out of the mine, just like that
come out, when even bureaucrat, I figure, scuffles
into the elevator doors, scuttles the lobby, fights

his trench-coat caught in the revolving doors.
I'd scumble them to the slagheap, powder them,
like bakers, but use a darker dust to let the mute
values of the chiaroscuro speak for the blast

of mother lodes silting to sludge in their lungs.
He shod them in *viscacha* hides, so they descend
looking up, look down on the way out, the broken
light on the ladder's rungs washing them the tint

of memory, the petty metalloids they haul
weighing with a dogma that says the jaundice
and the black-lung, the days sunk sorting
gangue from wealth, the bad payout and worse

pay-off is buildup to wildcat strikes first,
some cataclysmic, redemptive blow afterward.
I've tried translating the snarly syntax
and wounded vocabulary that had the leafy

Parisian chestnut turn and shed to show Peru
in all its interhuman and parochial squalor,
tried to figure if the poor were toppled by cholera
or just rehearsed their spite in foregone conclusions.

Vallejo, where I cooked, sometimes you'd see,
among the executive and broker, professors also,
those bruised egos who crammed you to a syllabus
to make a point. Tenured doyennes, interviewees

and junior faculty hoping for some crumbs.
You know they'd quote Baudrillard or Marx
while washing down their squab with claret,
quote even you maybe but could not see past

the drapes of the upscale Nuevo-Latino joint
your hobo still delousing, still foraging the dump;
could not think who plucked the bird or cooked the meal;
could not know the hecatomb that drove your heart,

how it happened in a dustbowl where a wife chased
the pent-up fowl, fried the scrawny thing, served it
in *rocoto* sauce, farmyard angels, you called them,
knowing a meal and thousand aches and no cure.

Fond

Reality is the great *fond.*
—Wallace Stevens

And the reality of *fond* is bone,
gathered last, way after the morning
steam of slaughter dissipates,

once the animals are quartered
turned rump and round tip;
blade, vacuum-packed; chuck, ground;

Three times a week they'll arrive,
femur and hip-bone clumped together
in the bag where fat seized.

Every other day, we roast them first.
Knuckles and shanks,
the stuff where play began

Homo ludens, being *ludens*
on a full stomach only, it follows
the blanched metacarpal remnants

of a meal would turn dice,
be cast and roll on that ground
that coupled play and luck,

where wagers pay sometimes,
where augur reads the great reality,
looming carnage, imminent downfalls.

They sizzle first, the smell rises.
When gristle swells, you'd hear first
a large pop, then a constant fizzle.

Also where dithyramb and psalm began,
the tibia hollowed out, drilled, carved
to pipe the wedding, pipe the cortege,

pipe the ritual where the lined-up oxen
fell, to the gods we say, knowing priest
might toggle an amulet out of his animal,

as long as we get a scrap.
For God the Duke of Guise sent
Coligny's head to Pope Gregory XIII

and began a craze that would obsolesce
the French word for butcher's shambles.
So stare enough at the great fond, reality begins

in the shambles, not the jumble
and confusion, though that might be it too,
the place where hides were drawn

to cover-up what happened inside.
Ax, knife, hacksaw process
the stuff we roast and caramelize,

empty into the stockpot and leave to a lazy
bubble to throw root ends and scraps in.
Back then a flea could down entire cities

and the charnel house was macro-cosmos
to the ditch, back then reality stole
the meaning words, and massacre,

the French for butcher's shambles
stepped-up to serious doings.
The poorest meal makes the best sauce.

Sustenance

i.

Maureen, the Lamaze teacher,
tucks the dummy of a newborn
in a white mesh drawstring sack
sewn on the bottom with a burgundy
velvet pillow ridged and grooved
with all the convolutions of the chorion
just to replicate a birth.

She turns the bag, undoes the string
and like a flight attendant at take-off
showing a mask drop like godsend,
lets the doll flop.
Easy, no tangled cords, no blood,
no time to worry the first gasps,
deft enough to move to the next topic:
double clamps, father's snips.

Some weigh the cost of banking
the left-over cells from the fresh-cut cord
to fend diseases in forty, fifty years.

I'm thinking lopped ears, sliced fingers,
dangling skin, thinking the stuff we slough
and how the class skimmed what every volume
in the small library of pregnancy and birth
my wife has poured through mentions:
those uterine contractions
so rile with pain, like all pain's cognates—loss,

bad falls, crashes—they're powerful enough
to re-christen, transubstantiate.
Not placenta, afterbirth; sustenance to waste.

Maureen has crumpled the empty sack.
Somebody wonders out loud, what happens
to all *that*, yes, *that* is the word she uses.

ii.

Sally, the yuppie yoga mom says
some people fertilize a new tree,
and she thought about it but reconsidered
on the grounds that Risdi, their retriever
likes to maw the compost pile already.

Helen, the hypno-birth, says
in the chat room of futuremom.com
someone told her she knew someone
who knew someone
who ate it.

Vestigial sea.
Holding tank.
Brine bag.
Transient organ.
Supposedly the place instinct sends us to
when we sense danger, when we fear.

The place grandparents go to
when mind and body have u-turned
and backtracked far enough
senility makes them primordial.

Maureen assents, in some cultures
the placenta is seen as sacred
chalice, host, sap, wine,
in some cultures they do eat it.

iii.

Think how the meadow rolls,
how the priest steps in.
What exactly did he do?

In the poem, in Homer
he led the victim to the altar
scattered grain on its neck
felled ox, goat or sheep
to observe the shares of gods
men, beasts.
         In prose, in Lucian,
he stands like an ogre, carves,
pulls entrails, digs out the heart
and *spills the blood about*
the altar, in a precinct ill
supplied with water, where
ugly piles of offal build up
to feed clouds of flies,
packs of mongrels.

What else is a poem but
the elisions that re-pay gifts
or explain the take-backs?
What else but ludicrous plots
to figure out the ambiguous blessings
the deceptive arrangements
in which we have no say
because they are buried
so deeply in us we chalk
them up to the gods?

Why not turn flesh invisible;
make the word incarnate?

iv.

"How would you cook it?" My wife whispered.

The tripe you layer with aromatics,
pack tightly, cover with white stock and braise.

The whole liver, wrap in caul fat and roast.

Acidulate the blood otherwise it clots.

The spleen "beautifully symmetrical"
says one cookbook is seasoned,
stuffed and rolled.

In some religions then
blanquettes of saints, roulades of sinners
working the dense brush, the murky plateaus,
the involved byways, the sheer walls
in the climb to nirvana.
Crags are eras there;
Lapses, the only landmarks.

Terrines of the next Dark Age.
Ballotines of an upcoming Renaissance.

The question lingers:
what happens to all *that*?

V.

I'd imagined the moth-wing haze,
the gauze light of parlors ribbed
by a floriated vascular exuberance,
at worst the sheer pantyhose
crumpled on the floor, insubstantial.

My wife has the presence of mind
to call me from the warming table
where baby clenches her first fist
to see it, the stuff I spent months
meditating into drafts, vestigial sea,

brine sack, chalice, sap. More silver
skin than lacquer, what skin there is
to see when the midwife lifts
and stretches it like stubborn dough,
she calls it beautiful, beautiful.

I've smelled its smell, in hospitals,
but also early mornings when the truck
backed-up to the ramp and the driver opens
his doors and lets the slaughterhouse
whiff from his delivery into prep.

vi.

Splayed in the pan,
deflated chalice, drained sea,
the glint of fresh accident,
the spongy deadweight of all insides,
ready for the lab where they check it
and then toss it in the red bin with
all the other biohazard waste.

Though we worried it,
the kicks and turns inside,
dog-eared the guides and brochures
highlit *previa* or *abrupta* like splits in dogma,
worried the dimples in the white-noise
of the ultrasound and the spectral, tidal flesh there.

What imagination does with fact:
Turns body temple, the word incarnate,
forgets, at its most sublime,
with historiated initials, brushed ivy curling
on every page, like the bramble of sin you guess,
the *word* needed 800 sheep shorn,
slaughtered, skinned, stretched, scrapped,
800 to get from *In principio* to *Amen*.

I've seen their pluck, or the pluck of their kind,
how blood curdled as the water reached
its boiling point, how the lung, puffed
and exhaled to the heat, like the last jammed
signal from above or below, or wherever,
on hold, trying to stammer the ghostly functions
the ghostly transformation of slough to sustenance.

vii.

Elision's the wrong word
for what imagination does.

A numinous ultrasound splotch
incarnate now and here's my wife also:
nurse asks her how much she hurts,
rate the pain on a scale of one to ten,
one being nothing, ten being hit by a train,
yes, hit by a train. And to me, having seen
groan and grimace and pain being
the one ontological proof easy to quantify,
I'm betting she'll choose the locomotive.

But to my wife, the decimals between
hurts are moot, baby's in her arms.
She's so deep in the mix-up of flesh and spirit,
that perplexed, mystifying mishmash, nothing matters
and you'd know why imagination had to puff Eden's mire
with a lungful of God's breath.

Entelechy of the Soul

If the Chinese are right, and when we die
our soul burs to our name and wagers its
survival on each passing mention, caring
little if the nasal hum of prayer mauls
or gossip's detours whisper, then those few
days, after the doctor breaks the news,
when wife and children spin the Rolodex
to make arrangements, call family and friends,
just then, soul must be an exile in a hot-
town, wandering the streets of language
and thinking the high-life as it rides
back and forth, non-stop in the static
of a line and clings to that tenuous
present tense that tells where body lies,
that weird subjunctive people wonder in,
the *what would've happened otherwise*,
without cigarettes or booze or motorcycle.

Soul is not an embryo which hatches
in us and come our last gasp barters its
tired or broken shell for a radiance
not even the most finicky Raphael
could render. It ebbs with the breath-marks
speech leaves when sons or brothers speak
their eulogies beside a grave and afterwards
is damned to the intermittent brief life
of afterthought. But those moments
when gesture turns one a replica of long
gone mom or dad just prove the afterlife
that secret violence that makes everything

and makes sure everything's uncertain,
that kind of force that crushes one strata
under another, piles millennia beneath ice caps,
where forgetting takes place and only chance
can scrape the bedrock of memory, let name bubble up.

If so ink must be the salvo soul waits for,
the hiss of spray can, the printer's prattle,
the clatter of platen and roller, even if
the three line obit seems more short-notice
than news, even if the tagger's R.I.P.
is on walls to condemned buildings,
on fences kept standing by root, shot and branch,
where, daytime, gulls drop clam shells, swoop down
it's peaceful enough for them to begin and peck;
night, police will floodlight love-cars,
drug deals and the tag, memory's stealth which
looks like a snarl coming untangled, not bobbined
to a skein yet, just midway between kink and thread
like our body when it figures out it has tenant
ghosts inhabiting within coming undone, letting
something surface from the Heraclitean runnel
where every thread's tangle, every body, sluice.

Ex-Votos

The mason-jar Patricia Gomez gulped from
is larger than her head, too large to hold,
disproportionate, unless one consider
the superlatives by which to multiply
a "shitty day" when the cramps come
from the stuff that works oven grime
and sewer build-up eating at tissue.
Then the jar of lye left inexplicably
on Patricia's nightstand is just right,
rudimentary and out of whack but right.
Joaquin's horse reared. Concepcion pilfered
a plum rubbed to a polish with typhoid.
Javier was conscripted and shot.
Juan heard troops, ran, was caught.
They are all here, pried from their parish,
on tin or masonite and one could call
the strokes that captured them primitive,
but the dabs that got them there
more primitive still: the slapdash
outlines of bad luck, the haphazard
fill-in of deliverance, the kind of balance
that veers a jeremiad into grace.
Thanks to the Virgin of the Lakes,
she let the Garcias hear the kindling beams.
Thanks to St. Emiliano, he halted the team
before the hair-pin turn. Mario Montes
was the only logger who survived
the swollen river. His whole camp
shares the panel though, where they
reel off the timber, arms raised,

as if dying meant the moment
where one's in two places at once,
the literal here where all there is
is steadying oneself, a metaphorical
elsewhere that keeps us groveling.
The dead have diminutive red
crosses over their heads, shorthand
that makes survival mean a paragraph
chock-full of mistakes and two strokes
withheld, something so quickly brushed.

Graffiti

Out of reluctant matter
what can be gathered?
—Milosz

No one heard the nozzle spray the storefront wall,
        though it must've hissed like rumor ending
        someone, except, the someone here's a somewhere,
a block or neighborhood; the bad rep, the bramble
        of gang signs sprouting from a single wavy line,
        and the line's eventual fruit, the more elaborate
filled-in uncials, pen-names to the thugs or artists
        Major is fighting by putting murals all over the place.
        Still NEEHI and MUFF have climbed impossible
heights, water-towers, bridges, smokestacks, so the city,
        or at least, the stretch of it I commute
        seems the notepad to their nightly go rounds.
Illegible, like Carolingian print. Worse really,
        Carolingian print on a balloon, bowls distended,
        stretchers curved, serifs morphing like strung-up
reptiles. I used to think the angry flick that left its mark,
        sustained, would gather force to something
        more profound or precious, was embryo
to chapter and verse. From there, wear
        the Pampers of linear A, crawl on linear B
        and you're of to limn the Greek encampments,
the Trojan court, invent the gods; you're off, in short,
        to pry fortune's sting, heart's angry thrust.
        But I must be wrong about what rage will smudge to out.
No, no line or doodle. What the block woke up to
        on the braid shop's front wall was a priapic

dynamo, hoodie on, pants ruffled to the ankle,
jerking-off under a trellised arch of cursive that tells
    ·   the passer-by what exactly to suck on.
         If in doubt, follow the last minute arrow
that tails the S in THIS. The potter's score marks,
         a notch, a scratch to sign where clay
         should curve, widen or narrow, liminal really,
but noticed by the merchant who being merchant
         co-opted them, began his own nick and gash
         to track credit and debt, that's the quick rundown
to the genesis to well, name it, baby's block letters
         and Aeschylus, which makes writing more
         stretch-mark than embryo and with the merchant,
chiseling how many oxen he let go for a poor harvest,
         the open vein in the superstructure
         my Marxist friends love to mine daily.
I like to pair one of them, the one who's all Althusser
         and Jameson, the one who whishes the graffiti
         on his block were more "transgressive"
with the owner of the shop who, greeted by erect
         hoody hoodlum, had to drive 20 minutes
         to *Just Ask*, dole out the fifty bucks for pressure
washer and fork thirty more on chemicals just to spend
         the day scrubbing and hosing last night's
         transgressive fun out of a porous stucco.
Residue and vestige, the extant codicils, the squiggles
         with someone's whereabouts "CHULA WAS HERE,"
         the wisdom, advice, directive "SUCK ON THIS,"
In Memoriams, Lascaux, Fresco, the blurry traces
         of blood or spit, parchment, papyrus

maybe their lingering is a lucky ride on
mineral's stubborn thirst. Think about it, think the owner
a whole day going at the paint. He walks back,
does that connoisseur tilt just to see the onanistic
ghost still haunts his wall. Think about it, Linear A
linear B weren't meant to be preserved.
A fire kilned them. They're still open accounts.

Notes

"The Smell of Cooking" borrows much of its imagery from Braudel's *The Structures of Everyday Life*. The Shakespeare quote comes from *Anthony and Cleopatra*. Caesar's speech is not referring to the Pax Romana of course, but rather to the military virtues which Romans congratulated themselves for and which we keep praising. The Tu Fu quote comes from François Cheng's *Chinese Poetic Writing*.

"Expulsion" refers to Genesis 3:19.

"Honest" quotes from Wordsworth and Milosz.

"Dishwasher" quotes from Dean Young.

"Back Alley" quotes from Sor Juana and Alan Dugan.

"Surveillance" references and quotes primarily from Whitman's "Song of Occupations."

The historian in "Banquet" is Jacob Burckhardt. The grandee alluded to in the poem is one Francesco Coppola.

"Failed Vallejo Translation" alludes to various Vallejo poems, including "Los Mineros Salieron de la Mina," "Telurica y Magnetica" and "Gleba."

I owe the knowledge of etymological shift of the word massacre in "Fond" to David Riggs' *The World of Christopher Marlowe*.

In "Sustenance" the information on the 800 sheep comes from Peter Brown's *The Rise of Western Christendom*. The poem borrows from and alters several of Rodney Jones' poems.

Several writers proved invaluable in articulating my own experiences in the kitchen. At points I borrowed or quoted from them. The anecdote about the Roman feast in "The Smell of Cooking" comes from one of Michael Ruhlman's books. "Dishwasher," "Surveillance," and "Lockerroom" quote, borrow or alter passages from Anthony Bourdain's *Kitchen Confidential*.

Also Available from saturnalia books:

Days of Unwilling by Cal Bedient

Letters To Poets: Conversations about Poetics, Politics, and Community
edited by Jennifer Firestone and Dana Teen Lomax

Famous Last Words by Catherine Pierce
Winner of the Saturnalia Books Poetry Prize 2007

Dummy Fire by Sarah Vap
Winner of the Saturnalia Books Poetry Prize 2006

Correspondence by Kathleen Graber
Winner of the Saturnalia Books Poetry Prize 2005

The Babies by Sabrina Orah Mark
Winner of the Saturnalia Books Poetry Prize 2004

Polytheogamy
Poems by Timothy Liu / Artwork by Greg Drasler
Artist/Poet Collaboration Series Number Five

Midnights
Poems by Jane Miller / Artwork by Beverly Pepper
Artist/Poet Collaboration Series Number Four

Stigmata Errata Etcetera
Poems by Bill Knott / Artwork by Star Black
Artist/Poet Collaboration Series Number Three

Ing Grish
Poems by John Yau / Artwork by Thomas Nozkowski
Artist/Poet Collaboration Series Number Two

Blackboards
Poems by Tomaz Salamun / Artwork by Metka Krasovec
Artist/Poet Collaboration Series Number One

To the Bone was printed using the fonts Figural and Kabel.

www.saturnaliabooks.com